Bitter Grass

Also by Gëzim Hajdari, from Shearsman Books

Stigmata (translated by Cristina Viti, 2016)

Books in Albanian

Antologia e shiut, Naim Frashëri, Tirana 1990
Trup i pranishëm / Corpo presente, Botimet Dritëro, Tirana 1999
    (bilingual Italian/Albanian).
Poezi të zgjedhura 1990–2007, Besa 2008
*Gjëmë: Genocidi i poezisë shqipe, Mësonjëtorja, Tirana 2010

Books in Italian

Ombra di cane / Hije qeni, Dismisuratesti 1993, Supplement to issue
    n° 110 of *Dismisura*
Sassi controvento / Gurë kundërerës, Laboratorio delle Arti 1995
Pietre al confine, Associazione Culturale "E-senza" Metrica", Comune
    di Ancona, 1998.
Antologia della pioggia / Antologjia e shiut, Fara Editore 2000; 2nd edition,
    Edizioni Ensemble 2018
Erbamara / Barihidhët, Fara Editore 2001, 2nd edition, Cosmo Iannone
    Editore 2013
Stigmate / Vragë, Besa, 2002; 2nd edition, 2006; 3rd edition, 2016
Spine Nere / Gjëmba të zinj, Besa 2004; 2nd edition, 2005
Maldiluna / Dhimbjehëne, Besa 2005; 2nd edition, 2007
Poema dell'esilio / Poema e mërgimit, Fara Editore 2005; 2nd, expanded
    edition, Fara 2007
Peligòrga / Peligorga, Besa 2007
Poesie scelte 1990–2007, Besa 2008; 2nd ed., 2008; 3rd ed., 2014
Poesie scelte 1990–2015, Edizioni Controluce 2015
Corpo presente / Trup i pranishëm, Besa 2011; 2nd ed., Edizioni Controluce 2018
Nur. Eresia e besa / Nur. Herezia dhe besa, Ensemble, 2012
I canti dei nizam / Këngët e nizamit (i canti lirici orali dell'800). Besa 2012
*Evviva il canto del gallo nel villaggio comunista / Rroftë kënga e gjelit në fshatin
    komunist.* Besa 2013
Delta del tuo fiume / Grykë e lumit tënd. Edizioni Ensemble 2015

Gëzim Hajdari

Bitter Grass

translated from Italian
by Ian Seed

Shearsman Books

First published in the United Kingdom in 2020 by
Shearsman Books
1 Hicks Close
SHRIVENHAM
Oxfordshire
SN6 8FL

Shearsman Books Ltd Registered Office
30–31 St. James Place, Mangotsfield, Bristol BS16 9JB
(this address not for correspondence)

www.shearsman.com

ISBN 978-1-84861-703-2

ACKNOWLEDGEMENTS
Some of these translations first appeared in
The Fortnightly Review and *Poetry Salzburg Review.*

Erbamara / Barihidhët was first published in a bilingual
Italian / Albanian edition in Italy by Fara Editore, Rimini, in 2001;
a second edition was published by Cosmo Iannone Editore, Isernia, in 2013.

AUTHOR'S NOTE

Bitter Grass was written in 1976 while I was in my last year of high school in the city of Lushnjë in Albania. It was refused by N. Frashëri, the government publication house in Tirana. According to the censor, "the texts in this collection do not deal with the theme of our socialist village; the hero of the poems is a solitary person who flees from his contemporaries, from the Youth Association, from reality; moreover, the transformations that socialism has brought to the countryside under the guidance of the Party are entirely absent..." At that time, the collection had the title *The Forest Diary*. I translated the texts from Albanian into Italian in 1999. Two years later, in 2001, the work was published for the first time by Fara. This new publication has been expanded and includes new texts in respect to the first edition.

Offering these poems to readers, it's as if I were going back many years to the icy and inhospitable winter of the Albanian dictatorship where I began my journey as a poet.

—Gëzim Hajdari, *Bitter Grass*
(*Erbamara*, Cosmo Iannone, 2013)

TRANSLATOR'S INTRODUCTION

Gëzim Hajdari was born in 1957 in the mountain village of Hajdaraj, in the province of Lushnje in the west of Albania. He came from a family of landowners whose property was confiscated during the communist dictatorship of Enver Hoxha.

After graduating in Albanian Language and Literature at the A. Xhuvani University in Elbasan in 1990, he worked in a variety of jobs while being intensely involved in journalism and political activism. In 1992 he fled to Italy after repeated threats because of his outspoken criticism not only of the abuses perpetrated by the former communist powers but also those of the post-communist government.

Upon arriving in Italy, Gëzim Hajdari worked in a number of manual jobs and initially occupied the ruins of an abandoned building in Frosinone near Rome. In 1993 a bilingual Italian / Albanian edition of poetry, *Ombra di cane / Hije Queni* (Dog's shadow), was published by Dismisuratesti. Hajdari values equally his mother-tongue and the language of his adopted country, and writes in both. Under the Albanian communist government, the study of the Italian language was banned because of Italy's 1939 occupation of Albania.

However, as Hajdari informs us:

> Alongside the official culture, another clandestine literature was also circulating. We read Italian authors that were seen as 'decadent' by the official communist culture. The texts by these authors were secretly copied by hand to escape censorship, because it was easy enough to end up in prison for subversive propaganda against the culture of 'socialist realism'. It was in this way that I read Dante, Petrarch, Boccaccio, Ariosto, Tasso, Catullus, and other foreign classics secretly translated into Albanian. Reading these great poets made me fall in love with the Italian language. In the remote, icy winter of the Albanian dictatorship, my dream was to be able one day to read the *Divine Comedy* in the original language.[1]

---

[1] See Cristina Viti's 2016 interview with Gëzim Hajdari at https://www. wordswithoutborders.org/dispatches/article/an-interview-with-gezim-hajdari-cristina-viti. Accessed 30 August 2018.

Growing up in a family who loved languages and literature, Hajdari was encouraged to be curious about other languages and cultures. He started learning Italian from a neighbour in his village who had spent some time with an Italian road-building crew in the 1940s. When Hajdari arrived in Italy in April, 1992, he already had a good grasp of the Italian language, and began translating his poetry from Albanian into Italian during his initial years in Italy.

After the publication of *Ombra di cane*, Hajdari went on to publish a number of bilingual collections. In 1997 he was awarded the prestigious Eugenio Montale Prize, and following this was granted honorary citizenship of Frosinone and given an apartment. The bilingual editions are of vital importance:

> If we look back at history, we find that the forefathers of Albanian literature wrote in Latin and that their works were printed in Rome. By writing in Italian I am stimulating and enriching the Italian language, but also my original language. I write in Italian and torment myself in Albanian—and vice versa! This is not a question of bilingualism, but of one 'double language'. So my writing is a linguistic migration: to go in and out from one language to the other, teaching people to become migrants and foreigners so as to share common destinies and common futures. The language of the exiles returns a spark of truth to metaphor and vitality to language.[2]

As well as several volumes of poetry, Hajdari has published collections of essays and travel writing, including a book of reportage on his journey through war-torn areas of Africa, and a number of translations from Albanian into Italian. He gained a degree in Modern Letters from La Sapienza University in Rome in 2004. His work has been translated into several languages. *Stigmata,* translated by Cristina Viti, was his first collection to appear in English, published by Shearsman Books in 2016.

Hajdari also promotes the enrichment of poetry from different languages and cultures through his work as an editor. Since 2012 he has been the director of the Erranze series for the Italian publishing house Ensemble, which has brought out a number of collections in translation, with an emphasis on marginalised and exiled writers.

---

[2] See Cristina Viti's 2016 interview with Gëzim Hajdari.

Most of the poems in the current collection actually date from 1976, when Hajdari was still in his final year at high school. He translated them into Italian in 1999, and they were first published as a book, with some additional poems, by Fara in 2001. Besides being remarkable in their own right, these poems are important because, as Hajdari wrote to me in an email, they 'signal the beginning of my literary and spiritual path during the communist dictatorship's years of terror'. The main characteristics of these early poems – for example, a political commitment to human freedom, a compressed lyricism, a blurring of the boundaries between a geographical landscape and a visionary dreamscape, the merging of the physical with the spiritual – are to be found throughout his work to the present day. The poems in *Bitter Grass* were initially written with the title *The Forest Diary*, and indeed the poems are at times reminiscent of the first canto of Dante's *Inferno* where the narrator finds himself lost in the woods on a hill.

The atmosphere of oppression is palpable in these pages. Nevertheless, there is a sense throughout that ultimately it is the human spirit which will prevail. As Andrea Gazzoni puts it, 'The grass of the fields of Darsìa is bitter, but it is more real and will outlast the collective hallucination of power.'[3] The poems, while highly personal, also draw their nourishment from myth, folklore and from different religions, which in Hajdari's view must come together to sustain us, rather than be in conflict with one another:

> The Albanian oral tradition is rich in original elements, blending and harmonizing the spirit of three religions: Islam, Christianity, and the mystical tradition of the bektashi Sufi. And it was folk song that kept the nation's collective memory alive during the dark, tragic moments of Albania's history.[4]

Hajdari was brought up in the epic tradition of poetry (his father knew more than ten thousand epic verses by heart), and we should note that Hajdari does not see his books as separate from one another, but rather as part of an epic poem which he is continually in the

---

[3] See Andrea Gazzoni's essay 'Monumento dell'erba amara', in *Erbamara*.
[4] See Cristina Viti's 2016 interview with Gëzim Hajdari.

process of writing. *Bitter Grass* marks the beginning of that long epic in progress.

It is hoped that this translation, alongside Cristina Viti's translation of *Stigmata*, will help bring the work of Gëzim Hajdari to a wider English-speaking audience.

Ian Seed,
December 2018

*

Nessuno sa se ancora resisto
in quest'angolo di terra arsa
e scrivo a notte fonda ubriaco
versi gioiosi e tristi.

Sogno la morte ogni volta
che torna la primavera.
I gemiti si perdono piano piano
nella nudità della pioggia.

Come brucia in fretta
la mia giovinezza senza richiami.
Ovunque dintorno mi sorridono
rose e coltelli.

Di fumo e alcool
odora così presto il mio corpo.
Chissà quale strana sorte un giorno
stroncherà la mia voce.

*

No one knows if I still hold out
in this corner of the burnt earth
and drunk in the deep night
I write joyous and sad lines.

I dream of death each time
spring returns.
Moans fade softly softly
in the nakedness of rain.

How fast my youth
burns without recall!
Roses and knives
smile all around me.

So soon my body
smells of smoke and alcohol.
Who knows what odd fate
will one day tear out my voice.

*

Mi troveranno nei campi trebbiati
senza respiro tra le labbra,
sdraiato sulla paglia che adoravo
con i colombi che beccano accanto.

Sul volto il fazzoletto bianco di mia madre,
mi porteranno nella stanza natale:
'Povero ragazzo, quanto ha sofferto!'
dirà la gente intorno al mio corpo.

Dopo avermi lavato
con l'acqua fresca del pozzo,
mi metteranno sul carro del grano
tirato dai buoi di campagna.

Percorrerò per l'ultima volta
la strada dove correvo nell'infanzia.
Se sarà al crepuscolo, le lucciole illumineranno
l'abisso della nuova dimora.

*

They will find me in the threshed fields
without a breath between my lips,
laid out on the straw I adored
with the doves pecking near me.

With my mother's white handkerchief over my face
they will carry me into the room where I was born:
'Poor boy, how he suffered!'
the people around my body will say.

After washing me
with fresh water from the well,
they will put me on the grain cart
pulled by country bulls.

For the last time I will go
along the road where I ran as a child.
If it's dusk, the fireflies will light
the emptiness of a new dwelling.

*

Anche nell'aldilà mi suonerà
la maledizione all'alba:
'Non avrai mai fortuna, che tu possa morire
per strada, come un cane!'

Ricorderò con timore
il mio dio crudele,
la melagrana spaccata
sotto la luna piena.

L'anatra che si tuffava nel lago,
i tori insanguinati.
Come un segno lugubre
il richiamo della volpe nel buio.

Gli stornelli che scavavano nella roccia
come se fossero impazziti,
le spine nere che cacciavo con l'ago
dai piedi di mia madre.

*

Even in the beyond I will hear
the curse at dawn:
'You will never be lucky. May you die
on the road like a dog.'

I will remember with dread
my cruel god,
the pomegranate split open
under a full moon.

The duck which plunged into the lake,
the bloodied bulls.
Like a funereal sign
the call of the fox in the dark.

The starlings that dug into the rock
as if they'd gone mad,
the black thorns I took out
of my mother's feet with a needle.

*

Ora vago tormentato nel paese
come uno spirito accoltellato.
Non mi fa più paura la morte,
né il freddo della sera.

So chi mi ha amato
nella collina delirante.
Un amore eterno:
il fango e il buio invernale.

Dietro le spalle m'insegue
come ombra il destino.
Tra i calmanti notturni scelgo
il veleno della vipera.

Due cose porterò con me
nel paradiso promesso:
i pianti in primavera delle prede
e i canti dei gitani.

*

Now I wander tormented through the country
like a spirit which has been knifed.
Death no longer makes me afraid,
nor the cold of evening.

I know who has loved me
in the delirious hills.
An endless love:
the mud and dark of winter.

Like a shadow my destiny
follows behind.
For a sleeping pill I choose
the poison of the viper.

Two things I will take with me
into the promised paradise:
the cries of the hunted in spring
and the songs of gypsies.

*

Nulla albeggia
sul volto del tempo.

Come una pelle nera
la notte balcanica.

Nell'abisso della valle
polvere i miei desideri,
cenere le mie stagioni.

Cosa cerco
in cima alla collina buia
di un paese tormentato
e di ubriachi?

Fuori, nel giardino, il vento
fa cadere le cotogne nel fango
come brutti sogni.

*

Nothing comes to light
on the face of time.

The Balkan night
is a black skin.

In the valley's depths
my desires are dust,
my seasons ash.

What am I looking for
at the top of a dark hill
in a tortured place
full of drunks?

In the garden outside, the wind
brings down the quinces into the mud
like bad dreams.

*

Gli anni si sciolsero,
ad uno ad uno si persero.
A stormi le rondini
nei cieli volarono.

Nel cortile lasciarono
piume e richiami.
Sulle grondaie delle casette
nidi e rumori.

Altri anni giunsero
di tuoni e gioia.
Altri voli di rondini
abbandonarono i nidi.

Nelle colline di Darsìa,
di buio e freddo,
invano attendiamo
una chimera all'orizzonte.

Le primavere fuggirono,
per gli abissi gocciolarono.
Come i cieli grigi
anche noi invecchiamo.

*

The years melted away,
disappeared one by one.
Swallows flew
in flocks in the sky.

They left their feathers
and calls in the courtyard,
nests and noises
in the gutters of small houses.

Other years brought
peals of thunder and joy,
other swallows in flight
abandoned their nests.

In the dark and cold
hills of Darsìa,
we wait in vain for a chimera
to arrive on the horizon.

The Spring seasons fled,
dripping into emptiness.
Like the grey skies
we too grow old.

*

O bosco darsiàno,
come allora m'incanti
con il nero silenzio,
voci e grida.

Spesso mi sgomentava
il tuo buio
negli anni dittatoriali
della mia infanzia.

Quando scendeva la sera
e smetteva il cuculo,
dalla tua notte comparivano
gli artigli del falco.

Dopo tanto tempo
appari come defunto.
La luna tra gli alberi,
come un occhio funebre.

Spogliato delle foglie,
dintorno niente grida.
Nei sentieri suonano
echi di spari.

Anche il mio nome,
scolpito sul tronco
come antica maledizione,
a metà è rimasto.

Ora cresci dentro di me,
nelle vene e nella carne.
Le tue ombre e gli spari
abitano il mio essere.

*

Ah, woods of Darsìa
how you put a spell on me
then with your black silence,
voices and cries.

In my childhood
in the years of dictatorship
how your darkness
would make me afraid.

When evening fell
and the cuckoo stopped calling,
a hawk's claws
came out of your night.

After so much time
it's as if you were dead,
the moon between the trees
like a funereal eye.

Stripped of leaves,
no sound around.
Then from the paths
the echo of shots.

My name too,
carved on the trunk,
has half-remained
like an ancient curse.

Now you grow inside me
in my flesh and veins.
Those shots and shadows
live inside me.

*

Immensa come te, collina,
è la mia angoscia.
Ogni verso ardente che m'ispiri
è amore e tormento.

Non sono stato mai così libero
come nella tua cima con i *xhin*.
Ricordo sempre che sono creazione
del tuo peccato selvaggio.

Fuggono all'istante dal freddo
sogni e speranze nel nulla.
Regni di passioni e rovine
invitano il mio corpo.

Dietro l'albero d'ulivo
chiama la mia ombra.
Una fiamma oscura all'orizzonte
brucia grida e voci.

*

Immense like you, hill,
is my dread.
Each scorching line you inspire
is love tormented.

I have never been so free
as on your peak with the *xhin*.[1]
I still remember I am born
of your wild sin.

Dreams and hopes flee straightaway
from the cold into nothingness.
The reign of passion and ruin
invites my body into it.

Behind the olive tree
my shadow calls.
A dark flame on the horizon
burns voices and cries.

---

[1] *Xhin*, pronounced 'gin', are malevolent spirits which come out at night
and have a supernatural power over people and things. The legend comes
from Albanian fairy tales of Darsìa, but the word *xhin* is also related to the
Arabic *djinn*, and thus has connotations of 'genie' and other supernatural
creatures of Arabic literature. (Author's note.)

*

Appoggiati al muro della casetta,
nell'ultimo giorno d'autunno,
prendiamo il sole che piccchia,
io e una lucertola senza coda.

Nulla accade in questa provincia,
gli stessi uomini, gli stessi volti.
Tutto si trascina con fatica
nel fango incanutito da secoli.

D'ora in poi, nell'arena del gelo,
ci sentiremo soli nella collina cupa.
Io e il falco combatteremo
con i denti e gli artigli.

Sdraiato sulla terra umida
assaporo l'erbamara dei prati.
Negli abissi dei cieli impazziti
si perde il mio sguardo.

Non lontano dalla mia dimora,
dove si fecondano i fulmini,
il vento del mare porta come misericordia
i gemiti degli internati nei Campi.

*

Leaning against a small house
on the last day of autumn
I and a lizard without a tail
soak in the beating sun.

Nothing happens round these parts –
same people, same faces.
Everything drags itself through mud
whitened by centuries.

From now on, in this chilly arena
we'll be alone on the dark hill.
The hawk and I will fight
with tooth and claw.

Lying on the damp earth
I savour the fields' bitter grass.
My gaze is lost in the emptiness
of crazy skies.

Not far from where I live,
fertile for storms and lightning,
the sea wind carries like a call for mercy
the moans of those interned in the Camps.[2]

---

[2] The concentration camp for prisoners from the city of Lushnje. This was one
of the most brutal prisons for those charged with political crimes. One of nine-
teen such camps in Albania. (Author's note.)

*

Condannato da secoli nel fango
chiamo il mio dio misericordioso.
Nessuno trovo in questa provincia
per condividere il dolore d'uomo.

Fuggono le stagioni spaventate
verso i sentieri di incendi e abissi.
Polvere e cenere del tempo,
cadono sulle mie appassite spalle.

Dove si nascondono i miei anni verdi?
Da collina a collina,
la pelle dell'infanzia perduta
suona e trema al vento.

*

Condemned by centuries of mud
I call out for my merciful god.
I can't find anyone in this place
to share the pain of a human being.

The frightened seasons flee
towards fire and emptiness.
The dust and ash of these times
fall on my withered shoulders.

Where do my green years hide?
From hill to hill, the skin
of a lost childhood
trembles and echoes in the wind.

*

Mai baciato una fanciulla
nella mia gioventù di allora,
abbracciavo alberi
in loro assenza.

*

Never kissed a girl
in my youth,
embraced trees
in their absence.

*

Ahimè,
la mia infanzia
divorata dai falchi di Darsìa.

*

My childhood
alas
devoured by the hawks of Darsìa.

*

(A Sandor Petöfi)

Quando torni tu, cicogna,
sull'olmo di casa mia, in Darsìa,
mi rammenti Petöfi,
figlio della steppa ungherese.

Solo tu, caro *aist*,
nella battaglia di Transilvania,
piangesti accanto al corpo
del poeta magiaro.

*

(To Sandor Petöfi)

When you return, stork,
to the elm of my home in Darsìa,
you make me think of Petöfi,[3]
son of the Hungarian steppes.

Only you, dear *aist*,[4]
in the battle of Transylvania,
wept next to the body
of the Magyar poet.

---

[3] Sandor Petöfi, the great Hungarian poet of the nineteenth century, lost his life in 1849 at the age of 26 in the battle of Segesvár (now Sighişoara in Romania), one of the Hungarian battles for independence against the Hapsburg empire. Hungarian national hero and poet. (Author's note.)

[4] Aist: stork in Hungarian. A bird held in great affection by Petöfi, and which recurs often in his poetry. (Author's note.)

*

Non m'interessa
quale sarà il mio destino.
Se c'è qualcosa di lugubre intorno
no, non voglio saperlo.

Ho vissuto così a lungo
nel mio terrore.
Ho vagato per Hajdaraj
come nella mia tomba.

So ciò che mi attende con ansia
dietro il velo del crepuscolo.
In un mondo di coltelli
non chiedo di salvarmi.

*

I'm not interested
in what my fate may be.
If something awful is close by,
no, I don't want to know about it.

I've lived for too long
with my terror.
I've wandered around Hadaraj[5]
as if inside my own tomb.

I know what awaits me with longing
behind the veil of dusk.
In a world of knives
I don't ask to be saved.

---

[5] Hajdaraj is the name of the village where the author was born. It is situated to the north-east of the city of Lushnje, in the province of Darsìa. (Author's note.)

*

Se vedete uno sconosciuto che fugge sotto la pioggia,
il viandante sono io.

Se incontrate un forestiero che vaga nella nebbia,
lo straniero sono io.

Se ascoltate un ubriaco che grida nel crepusculo,
l'esule disperato sono io.

Se troverete un uomo che parla con se stesso
in cima alla collina buia,
quell'uomo folle sono io.

*

If you see someone you don't know running in the rain,
I am the wayfarer.

If you meet a stranger wandering in the mist,
I am the foreigner.

If you hear a drunk shouting in the dusk,
I am the desperate refugee.

If you find a man talking to himself
at the top of a dark hill,
that madman is me.

*

Spesso a notte fonda
entra una strana voce nella mia stanza,
giunge sempre alla stessa ora
dal profondo di un pozzo scuro.

Siede accanto al mio letto
cupa e minacciosa.
Quante volte mi sono svegliato
in ansia e spavento.

'Non ti spaventare fanciullo –
mi repete ogni volta al buio –
le ombre che ti si affacciano nei sogni,
non sono che chimere.

Vivrai a lungo da guerriero
tra vipere e corvi.
Per compagni di viaggio avrai
solo spine e pietre.

Vai avanti per la tua strada,
non dar retta ai finti oracoli.
Il tuo seme di contadino
inciderà sul fango albanese.'

Poi si dilegua nel buio
del fondo del pozzo scuro,
per tornare ogni notte alla stessa ora
più cupa e minacciosa.

*

Often in the dead of night
always at the same time
from the bottom of a dark well
a strange voice comes into my room.

It comes to the side of my bed,
gloomy and menacing.
How many times have I woken
anxious and full of fear.

'Do not be afraid, child,'
it repeats each time in the dark,
'the shadows leaning over you in dreams
are nothing but chimeras.

You'll live for a long time,
a warrior among vipers and crows.
For travelling companions
you'll have thorns and stones.

Follow your own road,
pay no attention to fake oracles.
Your peasant seed will leave its mark
in the Albanian mud.'

Then it fades away
into the depths of the dark well,
only to return gloomier and more menacing
at the same time each night.

*

Nessuno saprà mai
cosa accadrà al mio mondo.
Insieme ai tuoni e ai fulmini
trascorro le notti invernali.

Mi guardo intorno. Tutto tace.
Il fango si unisce all'eterno.
Invano cerco qualcuno all'orizzonte
a cui affidare il mio destino.

Ombre lunghe mi avvolgono
mani, piedi e cervello.
Non so se avrò un futuro
in una stirpe severa e insanguinata.

*

No-one will ever know
what will happen to my world.
I spend the winter nights
in the company of thunder and lightning.

I look around. All is silent.
The mud is one with eternity.
In vain do I search for someone on the horizon
I would trust with my destiny.

Long shadows wrap themselves
around my hands, feet, brain.
How could I have a future
among a people so harsh and bloody?

*

Sogni svaniti all'alba
perché mi lasciate solo
con le spine del melograno?

*

Dreams vanishing at dawn
why do you leave me alone
with the thorns of the pomegranate?

*

Luna,
è fuggita anche questa stagione
senza un bacio
nella notte bianca.

Cielo,
è passato anche quest'anno
senza una ragione,
con la sete dei pozzi prosciugati
nelle nostra labbra nere.

Valle,
sta andando via anche questo secolo
come un toro abbattuto,
con il tempo che ci scivola tra le dita
e il canto del cuculo da collina a collina.

*

Moon
this season too has fled
without a kiss
in the white night.

Sky
this year too has passed
without a reason,
with the thirst of dried wells
on our black lips.

Valley
this century too is moving away
like a felled bull,
with time slipping through our fingers
and the call of the cuckoo from hill to hill.

*

Non disperarti
perché la valle è triste
e la selva senza richiami al crepuscolo.

Il vento fa alzare
le ceneri dei fuochi spenti
in cima alla collina buia.

Non disperarti,
ricordati che ti sono a fianco
nascosto nel verde.

*

Do not lose hope
because the valley is sad
and the wood without a call at dusk.

The wind raises
the ashes of spent fires
at the top of the dark hill.

Do not lose hope.
Remember I am by your side
hidden in the green.

*

Non piangere,
è il pettirosso che corre
sul ghiaccio del ruscello.

Presto fiorirà il mandorlo
e gli uccelli lirici ci canteranno
nelle vene.

Non piangere,
ho percorso la tua ferita
per raggiungerti.

*

Don't cry,
it's the redbreast that rushes
over the stream's ice.

Soon the almond tree will blossom
and the lyrical birds will sing to us
in our veins.

Don't cry,
I have crossed over your wound
to reach you.

*

Mia patria,
perchè quest'amore folle per te?

Tu mi hai fatto nascere
per essere la tua ferita.

Dove nascondermi sulla
collina brulla?

I miei versi m'inseguono
come vecchi assassini.

Ogni notte si rompe qualcosa
nel profondo del mio ghiaccio.

*

My country,
why this absurd love for you?

You gave birth to me
so that I could be your wound.

Where can I hide
 on the bare hill?

My verses follow me
like old assassins.

Each night something breaks
deep inside me under the ice.

*

Stasera voglio che qualcuno mi chiami dalle pietre,
stasera voglio andarmene dalla mia Darsìa
sotto la pioggia.

Voglio guardare in faccia il mio dio crudele,
stasera voglio che la terra beva il mio sangue rosso
e nasconda la mia ultima parola.

Stasera voglio chiudere con la mia patria.

*

This evening I want someone to call me from the stones,
this evening I want to leave my Darsìa
in the rain.

I want to look my cruel god in the face,
this evening I want the earth to drink my red blood
and hide my last word.

This evening I want to end it with my country.

*

Correre tra le ginestre fiorite dietro al cuculo,
ascoltare all'imbrunire il richiamo del pettirosso
immobile sul ramo spoglio del biancospino.

Rammentare la voce di quelli che partono,
confondersi con la leggera tristezza dei passanti
e con il profumo dei campi di grano maturo.

Scrutare la collina, le luci e le ombre,
il tremolio della linea sottile dell'orizzonte che brucia
anche nell'aldilà con i vostri occhi verdi.

*

To run after the cuckoo through the gorse in bloom,
to listen as dark comes to the call of the redbreast
motionless on the bare branch of the hawthorn.

To remember the voices of those who leave
as they mingle with the small sadness of passers-by
and with the scent of the ripe cornfield.

To scan the hill, its lights and shadows,
the trembling of the thin line on the horizon as it burns
even in the beyond with your green eyes.

*

Forse domani non ci sarò
nei campi incanutiti.
Come una nuvola mattutina
scomparirà il mio volto.

Si perderà la mia voce
e il richiamo quotidiano.
Orfani nelle selve
speranze e sogni.

Appesi al fiume
resteranno nomi e ombre.
In polvere e cenere
la mia ossessione.

Sul corpo crescerà
un nuovo biancospino.
Sotto l'erba tenera
il mio segreto.

Verranno i giorni di maggio
con ginestre e sole.
Come prima canteranno
l'usignolo e il cuculo.

*

Perhaps tomorrow I won't be
in these whitened fields.
Like an early morning cloud
my face will disappear.

My voice will be lost
with everyday memories,
hopes and dreams
orphaned in the woods.

Still hanging by the river
names and shadows will remain,
the one who obsessed me
dust and ash.

A hawthorn will grow
above the corpse,
my secret kept
under tender grass.

The days of May will come
with gorse and sunshine.
The nightingale and cuckoo
will be the first to sing.

*

Appeso ad un chiodo
lo zaino di scuola del villaggio,
una nuvola bianca si posa sul pioppo
squarciato dai fulmini.
Della mia dimora natale, in cima alla collina,
pian piano si perdono le tracce,
nel giardino dei melograni, dove partoriva la cagna,
non ho messo più piede.
Non possiedo nessuna foto
della povera casetta di pietra focaia
dove tremavo e mi alzavo di buon'ora.
Si è seccato anche il gelso rosso nella siepe,
tace il vecchio pozzo nel cortile;
le farfalle lo attraversanno mattina e sera,
per gli olmi vaga la furba civetta
che annuncia la pioggia o richiama il bel tempo.
Ahimè, vago dintorno e nessuno mi vede,
dagli ulivi si alzano stormi di neri uccelli
nelle loro ali pesa come un dolore
il grigio del giorno.

*

My village school satchel
hangs from a nail.
A white cloud rests on a poplar
torn by lightning.
At the top of the hill, all trace of my birthplace
is slowly lost.
I haven't set foot in the garden of pomegranates
where the dog gave birth.
I don't have any photo
of the poor cottage built from fired stone
where I trembled and woke early.
The red mulberry tree in the hedge has dried,
and the old well is silent in the courtyard
crossed by butterflies morning and evening.
A clever owlet roams the elms
announcing rain or recalling fine weather.
I wander around and nobody sees me.
A flock of dark birds rises from the olives,
the day's grey in their wings
heavy like a pain.

*

I miei occhi, notte nera
dove bevi solo tu.

I miei occhi, giardino di sabbia
dove soffi solo tu.

I miei occhi, finestre spalancate
dove gridi solo tu.

I miei occhi, porto abbandonato
dove parti solo tu.

*

My eyes, dense night
where you alone drink.

My eyes, garden of sand
where you alone whisper.

My eyes, windows open wide
where you alone cry out.

My eyes, abandoned port
where you alone are leaving.

*

Il mattino imbiancato di rugiada,
camminiamo nel bosco senza un'anima.
Il profumo delle foglie gialle
risveglia in te un'infanzia lontana

In mezzo ai fitti rami platani
per prima tu trovi il sentiero.
Nella tua fronte e nelle tue mani
migrano tortore e merli.

I tronchi degli alberi spezzati
li conti con le dita, in silenzio.
Le loro fattezze rammenti
come fossero dei cari estinti.

Intristiti dagli echi e dalle voci di allora,
camminiamo in silenzio.
Sotto i nostri piedi giacciono
voci, lamenti e magie nere.

I tuoi occhi umidi di autunno
annunciano fughe e oblìo.
Persi nel bosco notturno
non troviamo la via del ritorno.

*

The morning whitened with dew,
we walk in these woods without a soul around.
The perfume of yellow leaves
reawakens your faraway childhood.

Among the thick branches of plane trees
you are the first to find the path.
Before your face and hands
ring-doves and blackbirds fly away.

Silently you count on your fingers
the trunks of fallen trees.
They are like loved ones who have died
whose features you remember.

Saddened by voices and echoes
from that time, we walk in silence.
Under our feet lie
those voices, moans and dark rites.

Your eyes moist with autumn
tell of flight and oblivion.
Lost in the night wood
we cannot find our way back.

*

Nello scorrere
del ruscello
ci dissetiamo,
io
e una colomba
innamorata.

*

In the flowing
stream
we quench our thirst
I
and a pigeon
in love

*

Dov'è la luna piena
gli stormi dei colombi bianchi?
Solo piogge e fango
mi circondano.

Tacciono le pietre sulla strada,
trema l'erbamara nei prati.
Sotto il cielo sempre cupo
alberi nudi, orfani.

Non più tra i sentieri
fischi lontani e suoni.
I sogni giovanili sono fuggiti
negli abissi degli anni.

Nulla è rimasto
nei luoghi natali di allora.
Tutto è svanito
e ricoperto dal buio.

*

Where is the full moon,
the flocks of white doves?
Only rain and mud
surround me.

The stones along the road are silent,
the bitter grass in the field trembles.
Under a sky always dark
naked, orphan trees.

No longer between the paths
far off whistles and sounds.
Dreams of youth have fled
into the abyss of years.

Nothing remains
of our homes back then.
Everything has vanished,
covered once more by dark.

*

Albeggia il vecchio pozzo in fondo al giardino,
sui rami del salice gli uccelli cantano di rado,
anche il secchio non suona più su e giù tra le pietre,
la corda assottigliata dalle mani si è spezzata.

Le voci e i passi dintorno si sono persi
e la stradina che ti porta lì si è coperta di malva.
Nello specchio d'acqua, come una volta,
invano attendo che appaia il volto di mia madre.

*

Dawn light on the old well at the bottom of the garden.
From the willow tree's branches, the birds rarely sing.
Even the bucket makes no sound up and down between the stones –
its rope worn thin has snapped.

Voices and the sounds of footsteps are lost
and the lane which has brought you here is covered in mallow.
In the water's mirror, I wait in vain just as I used to
for my mother's face to appear.

*

Peligòrga, caro uccello della valle,
a te i poeti di Darsìa
legavano il destino.

A te confidavano
pene e dolori,
nel tuo nido per terra
nascondevano i loro versi.

Quante volte li hai visti intristiti
nelle lunghe notti di tenebre.
Disperata gridavi all'orizzonte
per la loro sorte.

Ora sulle colline di Darsìa
si sono placati tuoni e fulmini.
Perché come trent'anni fa
temi ancora il destino dei poeti!

*

Peligòrga,[6] dear bird of the valley,
the poets of Darsìa
tied their destiny to you.

In you they confided
their pain and suffering,
hiding their verses
in your nest on the ground.

How many times you saw them
saddened in the long nights.
Their fate made you cry out
to the horizon.

Now on the hills of Darsìa
the thunder and lightning are placated.
Just as thirty years ago
you fear a poet's destiny.

---

[6] Peligòrga is a solitary green-feathered bird which frequents the borders of
rivers and streams. It nests in the earth, and can be found near Darsìa, the
hilly province where the poet was born. (Author's note.)

FIRST LINES

Lightning Source UK Ltd.
Milton Keynes UK
UKHW011452191219
355682UK00002B/237/P